Family

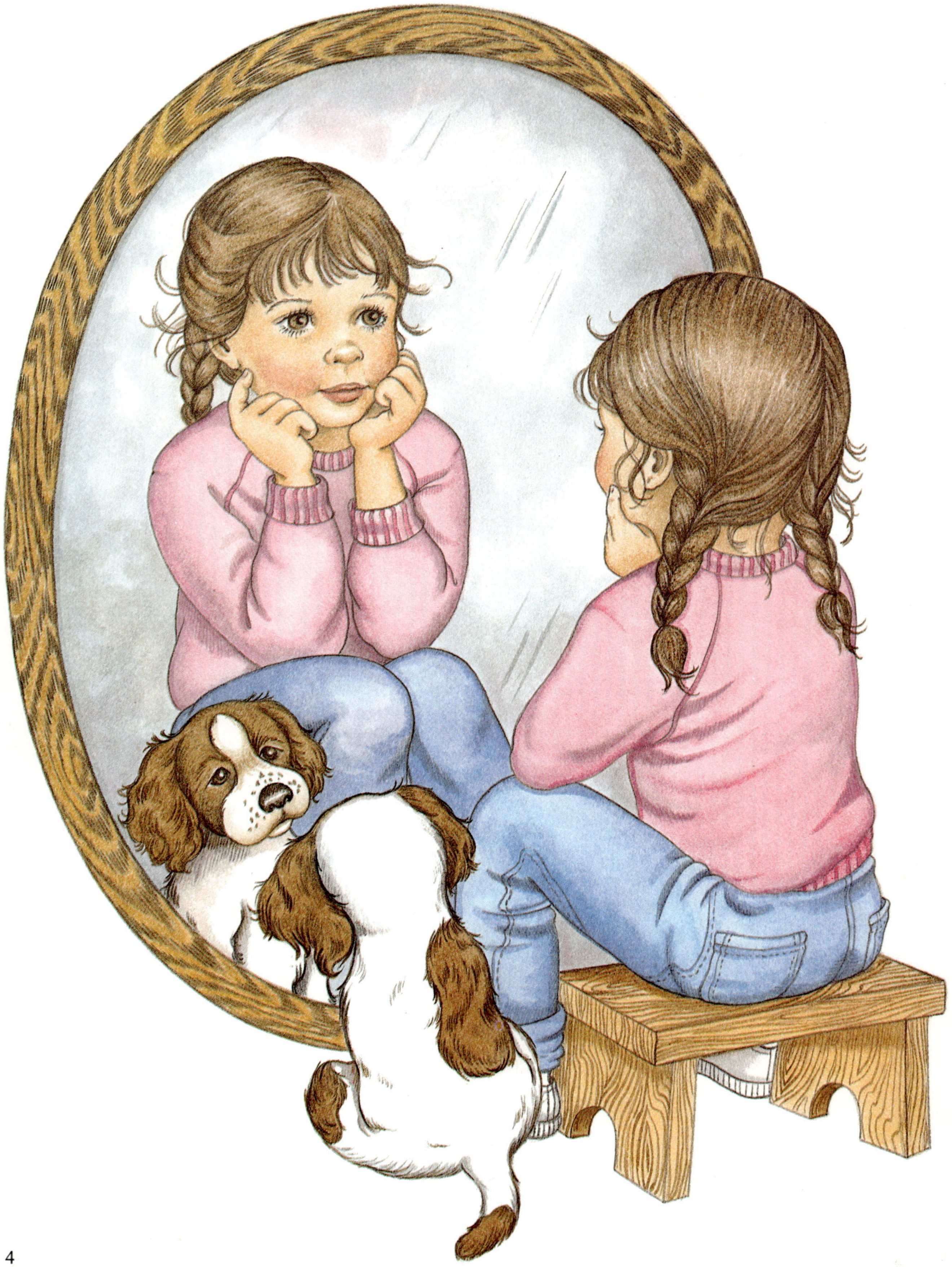

Family

FAVORITE POEMS

Between the dark and the daylight,
  When the night is beginning to lower,
Comes a pause in the day's occupations
  That is known as the Children's Hour.

—Henry Wadsworth Longfellow

illustrated by Linda Hohag
and Lori Jacobson

THE CHILD'S WORLD

ELGIN, ILLINOIS 60121

See page 32 for *Acknowledgements*.

compiled by Diane Dow Suire

Distributed by Childrens Press
Chicago, Illinois

Library of Congress Cataloging in Publication Data

Family / [compiled by] Diane Dow Suire ; illustrated by Linda Hohag.
    p. cm. — (The Shape of poetry)
  ISBN 0-89565-504-7
  1. Family—Juvenile poetry. 2. Children's poetry, American.
3. Children's poetry, English. I. Suire, Diane Dow, 1954-
II. Hohag, Linda. III. Series.
PS595.F34F34   1989
811'.008'0355—dc19
                                                  89-772
                                                    CIP
                                                      AC

©1989 The Child's World, Inc.
All rights reserved. Printed in U.S.A.

1 2 3 4 5 6 7 8 9 10 11 12 R 99 98 97 96 95 94 93 92 91 90 89

Everybody says
I look just like my mother.
Everybody says
I'm the image of Aunt Bee.
Everybody says
My nose is like my father's
But *I* want to look like *ME*!

— Dorothy Aldis

I HAVE a little shadow that goes in and out with me,
And what can be the use of him is more than I can see.
He is very, very like me from the heels up to the head;
And I see him jump before me, when I jump into my bed.

The funniest thing about him is the way he likes to grow—
Not at all like proper children, which is always very slow.
He sometimes shoots up taller like an India-rubber ball,
And he sometimes gets so little that there's none of him at all.

He hasn't got a notion of how children ought to play
And can only make a fool of me in every sort of way.
He stays so close beside me, he's a coward you can see;
I'd think shame to stick to mother as that shadow sticks to me!

One morning, very early, before the sun was up,
I rose and found the shining dew on every buttercup;
But my lazy little shadow, like an errant sleepyhead,
Had stayed at home behind me and was fast asleep in bed.

—Robert Louis Stevenson

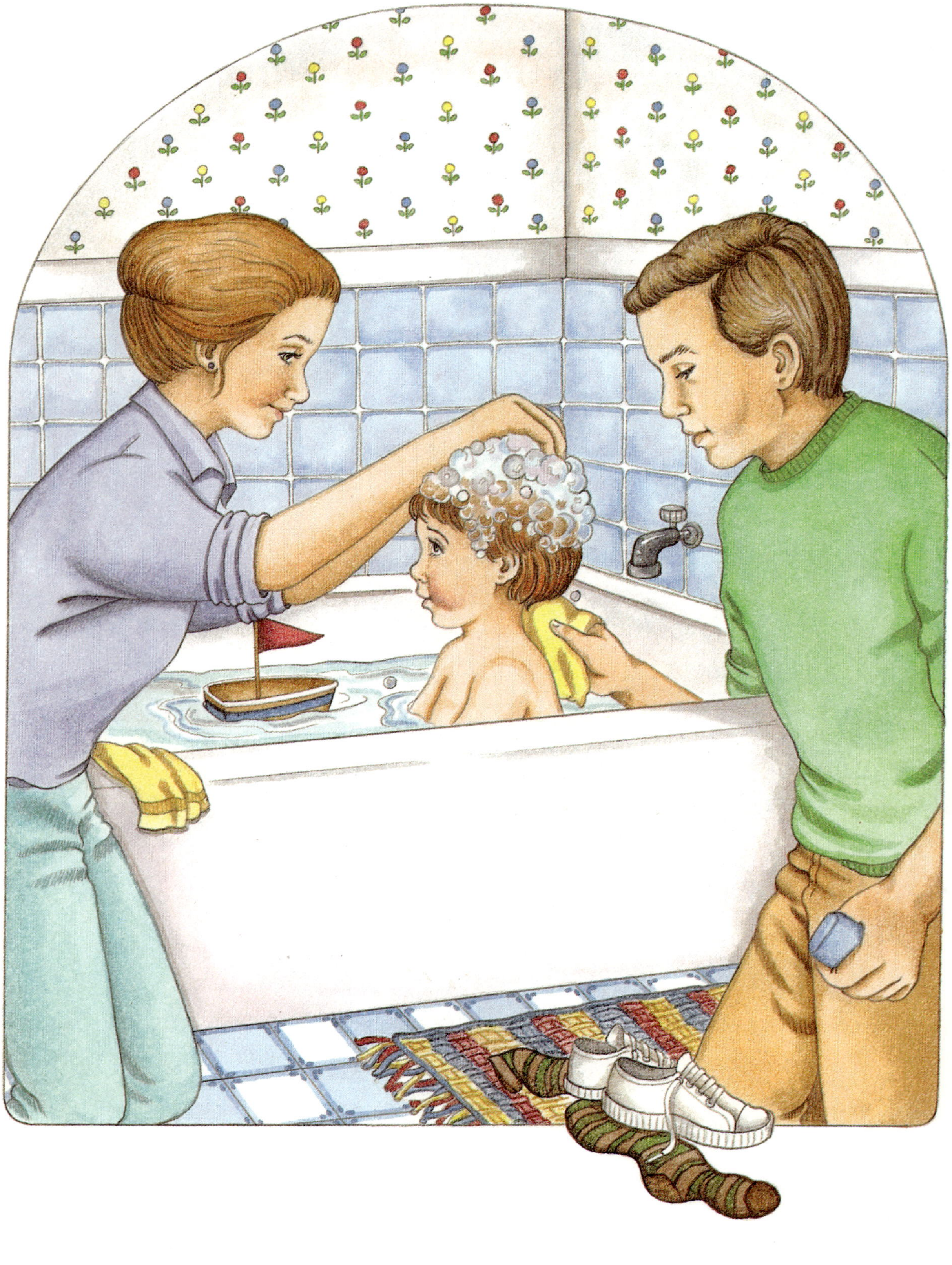

THE WAY they scrub
Me in the tub,
I think there's
      Hardly
      Any
      Doubt
Sometime they'll rub,
And rub and rub
Until they simply
      Rub
      Me
      Out.

—A.B. Ross

FATHER'S legs are very long.
He seldom walks for fun.
He mostly walks for getting there,
Which makes *ME* have to run.

—Aileen Fisher

MY LITTLE sister
Likes to eat.
But when she does
She's not too neat.
The trouble is
She doesn't know
Exactly where
The food should go!

—William Wise

THEY'RE big,
They're broad,
They're tall,
They're strong.
Their hands are large,
Their legs are long.
And no one tells them
What to do.
I wish I were
A grownup, too.

For then I'd live
Without a care:
I'd never have to
Comb my hair;
I'd never have to
Nap at noon.
I'd like to be
A grownup soon.

—William Wise

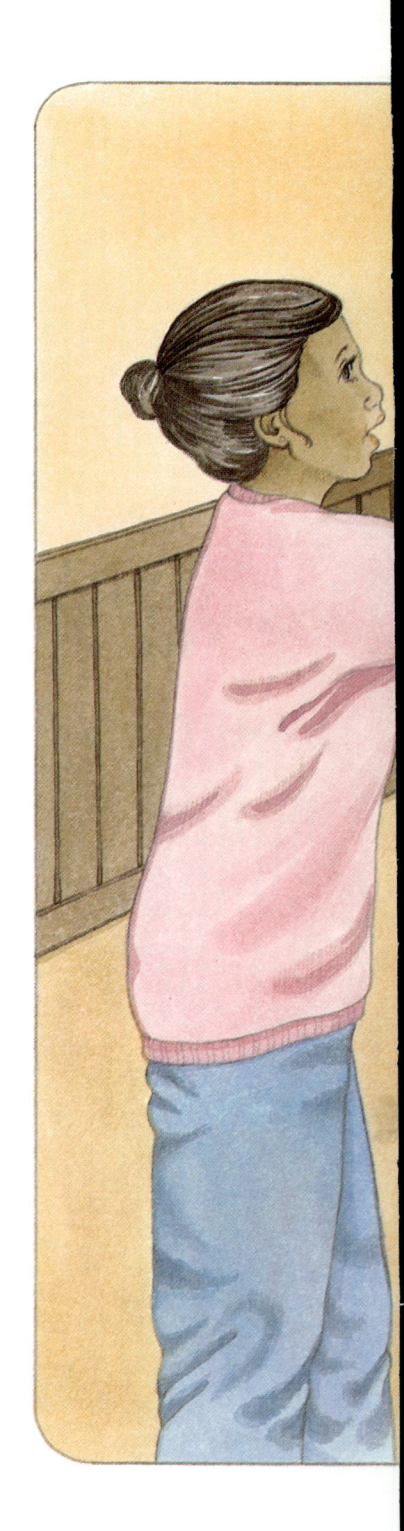

13

WHEN I grow up
(as everyone does)
What will become
of the Me I was?

—Aileen Fisher

IN go-cart so tiny
　　My sister I drew;
And I've promised to draw her
　　The wide world through.

We have not yet started—
　　I own it with sorrow—
Because our trip's always
　　Put off till tomorrow.

—Kate Greenaway

IF WE didn't have birthdays, you wouldn't be you.
If you'd never been born, well then what would you do?
If you'd never been born, well then what would you be?
You *might* be a fish! Or a toad in a tree!
You might be a doorknob! Or three baked potatoes!
You might be a bag full of hard green tomatoes.
Or worse than all that . . . Why, you might be a WASN'T!
A Wasn't has no fun at all. No, he doesn't.
A Wasn't just isn't. He just isn't present.
But you . . . You ARE YOU! And, now isn't that pleasant!

—Dr. Seuss

BIRTHDAY

In FORM and feature, face and limb,
   I grew so like my brother,
That folks got taking me for him,
   And each for one another.
It puzzled all our friends and family,
   It reach'd an awful pitch;
For one of us was born a twin,
   Yet not a soul knew which.

One day (to make the matter worse),
   Before our names were fix'd,
As we were being wash'd by nurse
   We got completely mix'd;
And thus, you see, by Fate's decree
   (Or rather nurse's whim),
My brother John got christen'd *me*,
   And I got christen'd *him*.

—Henry Sambrooke Lehigh

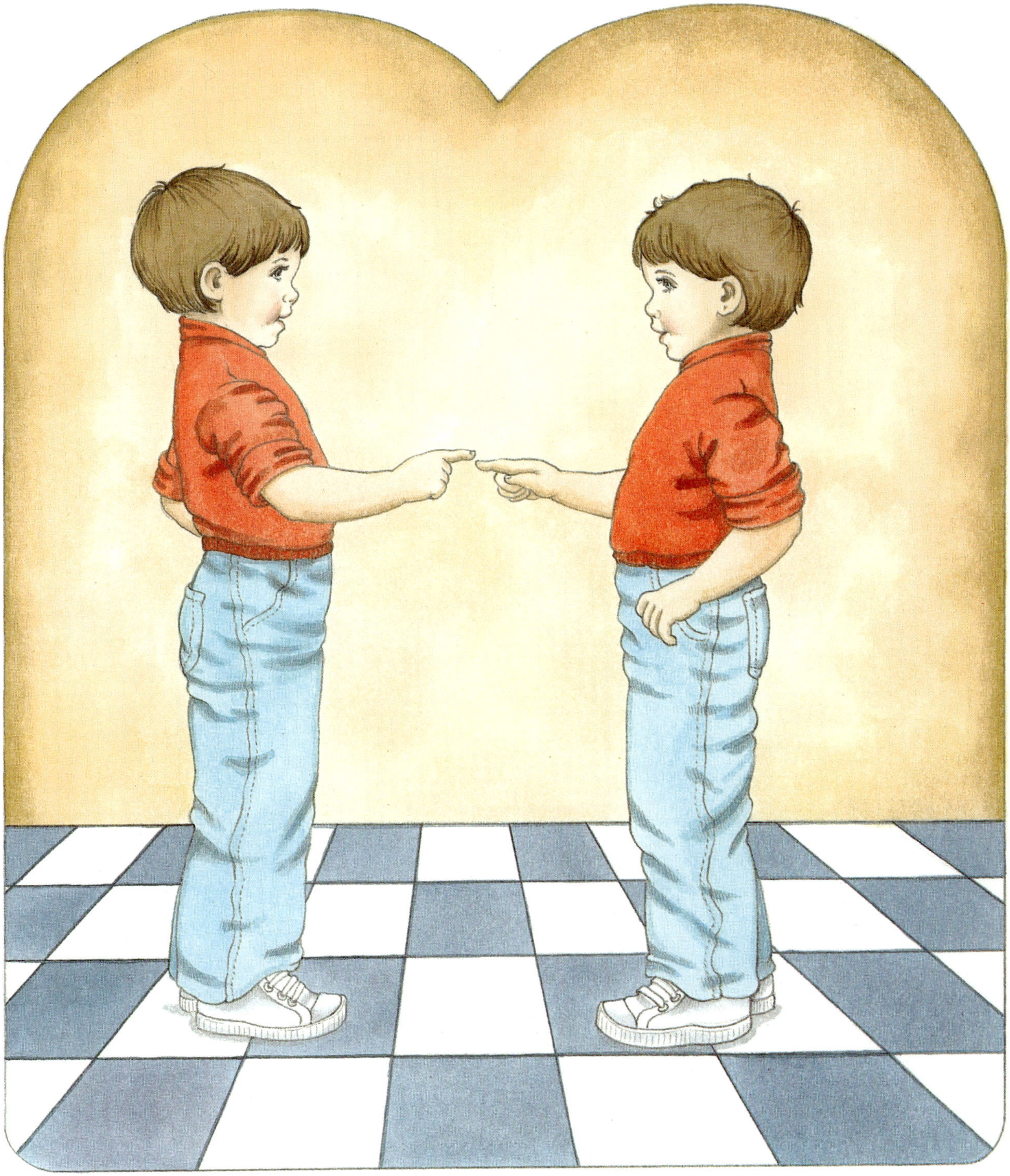

I KNOW a little zigzag boy,
　　Who goes this way and that;
He never knows just where he puts
　　His coat or shoes or hat.

I know a little zigzag girl,
   Who flutters here and there;
She never knows just where to find
   Her brush to fix her hair.

If you are not a zigzag child,
   You'll have no cause to say
That you forgot, for you will know
   Where things are put away.

—Unknown

My BROTHER is inside the sheet
That gave that awful shout.
I know because those are his feet
So brown and sticking out.

And that's his head that waggles there
And his *eyes* peeking through—
So I can laugh, so I don't care:
"Ha!" I say. "It's you."

—Dorothy Aldis

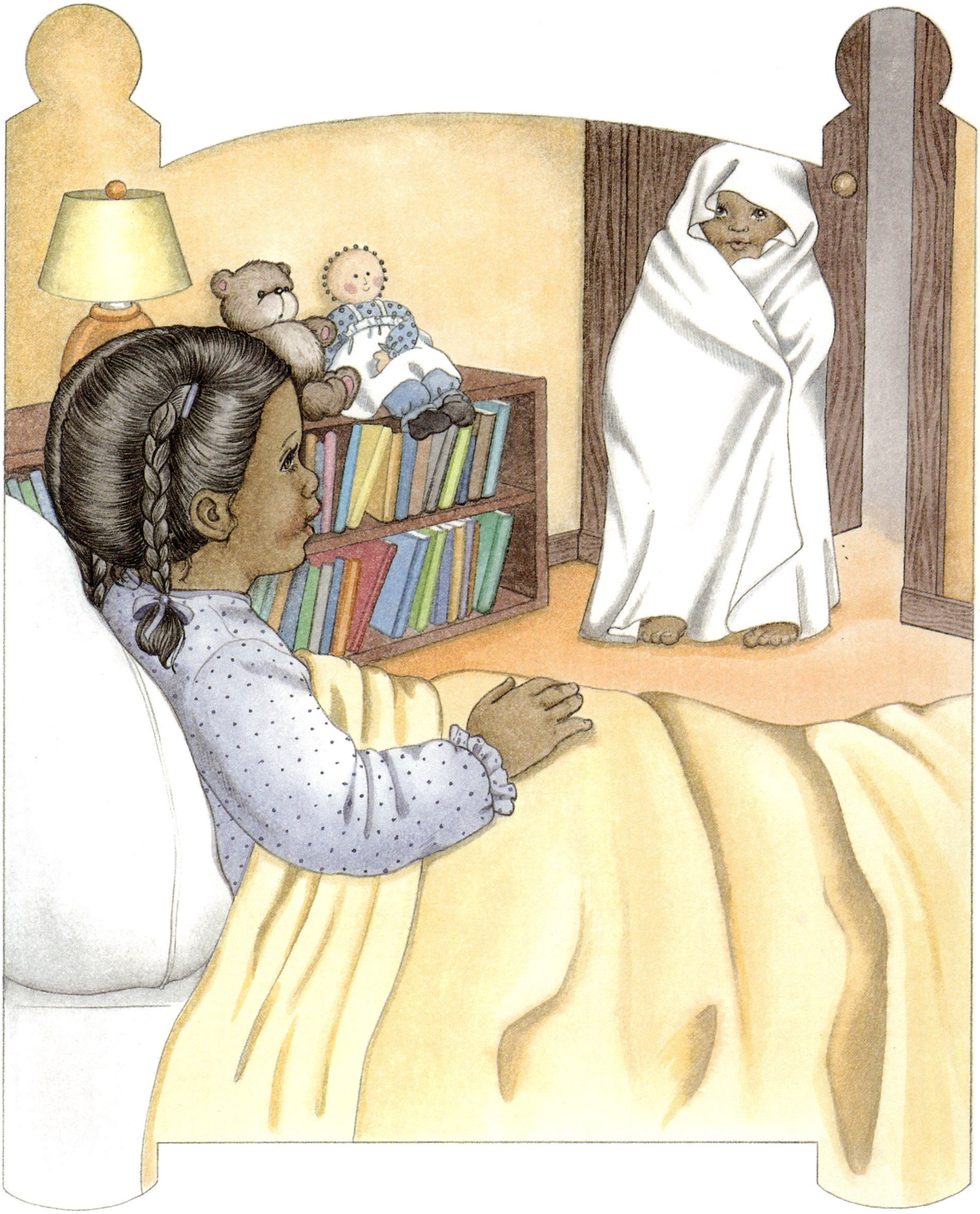

Tony said: "Boys are better!
　They can . . .
　　　whack a ball,
　　　ride a bike with one hand
　　　leap off a wall."

I just listened
　and when he was through,
I laughed and said:
　　"Oh, yeah! Well, girls can, too!"

Then I leaped off the wall,
　and rode away
With *his* 200 baseball cards
　I won that day.

—Lee Bennett Hopkins

25

FIVE minutes, five minutes more, please!
  Let me stay five minutes more!
Can't I just finish the castle
  I'm building here on the floor?
Can't I just finish the story
  I'm reading here in my book?
Can't I just finish this bead-chain—
  It *almost* is finished, look!

Can't I just finish this game, please?
   When a game's once begun
It's a pity never to find out
   Whether you've lost or won.
Can't I just stay five minutes?
   Well, can't I stay just four?
Three minutes, then? two minutes?
   Can't I stay *one* minute more?

—Eleanor Farjeon

AT EVENING when the lamp is lit,
Around the fire my parents sit;
They sit at home and talk and sing,
And do not play at anything.

Now, with my little gun, I crawl
All in the dark along the wall,
And follow round the forest track
Away behind the sofa back.

There, in the night, where none can spy,
All in my hunter's camp I lie,
And play at books that I have read
Till it is time to go to bed.

These are the hills, these are the woods,
These are my starry solitudes;
And there the river by whose brink
The roaring lions come to drink.

I see the others far away,
As if in firelit camp they lay;
And I, like to an Indian scout,
Around their party prowl about.

So, when my mom calls to me,
Home I return across the sea,
And go to bed with backward looks
At my dear Land of Storybooks.

—Robert Louis Stevenson

NIGHT is come,
  Owls are out;
Beetles hum
  Round about.

Children snore
  Safe in bed;
Nothing more
  Need be said.

—Henry Newbolt

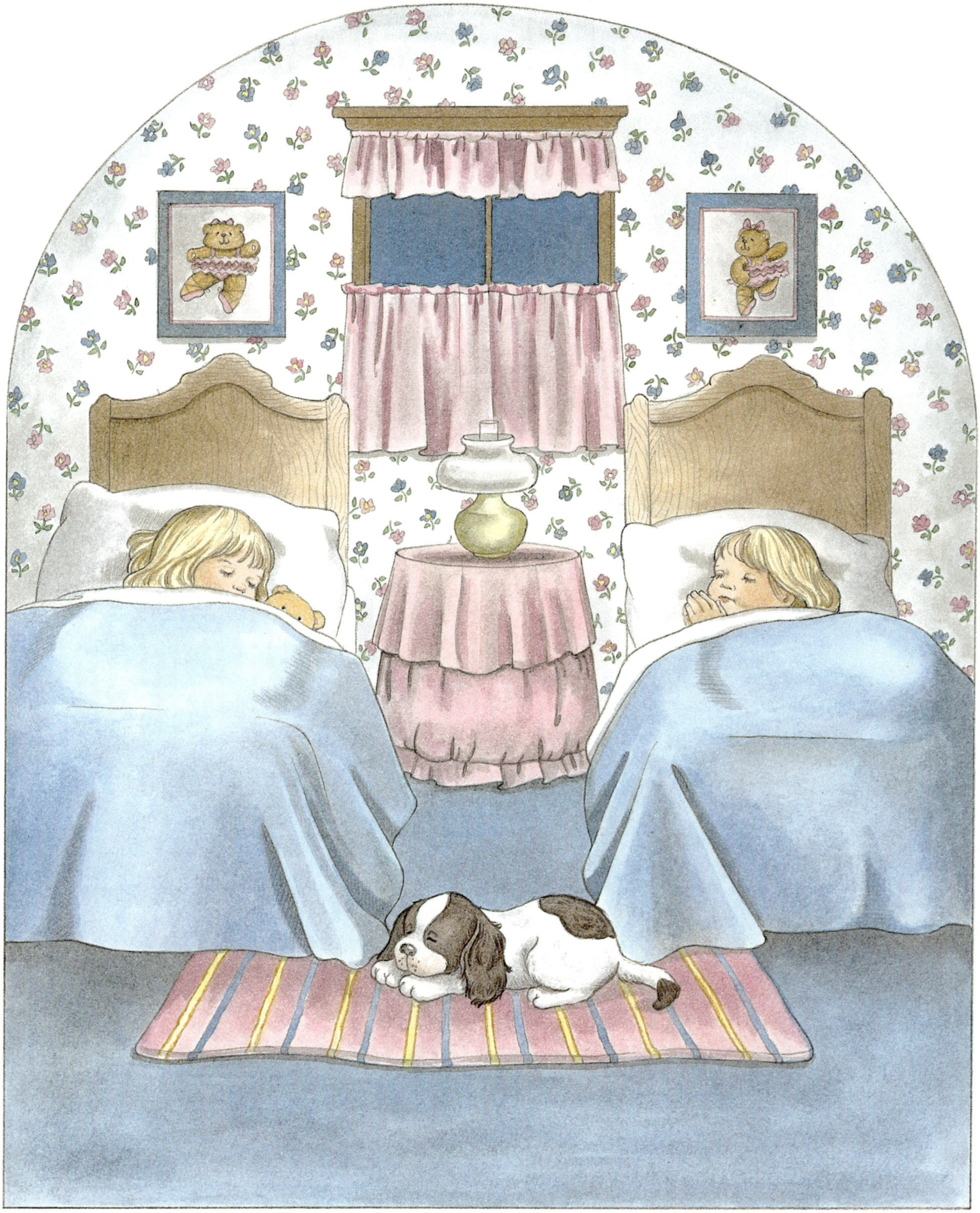

ACKNOWLEDGEMENTS

Every effort has been made to trace the ownership of all copyrighted material and to secure the necessary permissions to reprint these selections. In the event of any question arising as to the use of any material, the editor and the publisher, while expressing regret for any inadvertent error, will be happy to make the necessary correction in future printings.

Grateful acknowledgement is made to the following for permission to reprint the copyrighted material listed below.

"Everybody Says" (pg. 5) by Dorothy Aldis. Reprinted by permission of G. P. Putnam's Sons from EVERYTHING AND ANYTHING by Dorothy Aldis, copyright 1925-1927, copyright renewed 1953-1955 by Dorothy Aldis.

"Walking" (pg. 10) and "Growing Up" (pg. 14) from RUNNY DAYS, SUNNY DAYS by Aileen Fisher. Reprinted by permission of the author who controls rights.

"My Little Sister" (pg. 11) by William Wise from ALL ON A SUMMER'S DAY, © 1971. Published by Pantheon Books. Reprinted by permission of the author who controls rights.

"Grownups" (pg. 12) by William Wise from JONATHAN BLAKE: THE LIFE AND TIMES OF A VERY YOUNG MAN, © 1956, 1984. Published by Alfred A. Knopf. Reprinted by permission of the author who controls rights.

"If We Didn't Have Birthdays," (pg. 16) from HAPPY BIRTHDAY TO YOU! by Dr. Seuss. Copyright © 1959 by Dr. Seuss. Reprinted by permission of Random House, Inc.

"My Brother" (pg. 22) by Dorothy Aldis. Reprinted by permission of G. P. Putnam's Sons from HOP, SKIP AND JUMP by Dorothy Aldis, copyright 1934, copyright renewed © 1961 by Dorothy Aldis.

"Girls Can, Too" (pg. 24) by Lee Bennett Hopkins from GIRLS CAN, TOO, copyright 1972, Lee Bennett Hopkins. Published by Franklin Watts. Reprinted by permission of Curtis Brown, Ltd.

"Bedtime" (pgs. 26-27) from ELEANOR FARJEON'S POEMS FOR CHILDREN by Eleanor Farjeon. (J. B. Lippincott). Copyright 1933 by Eleanor Farjeon. Renewed © 1961 by Eleanor Farjeon. Reprinted by permission of Harper and Row, Publishers, Inc.

"Day's End" (pg. 30) by Henry Newbolt. Copyright owned by Francis Newbolt.

ORANGE COUNTY SCHOOL BOARD
PURCHASED WITH
ECIA CHAPTER 11 FUNDS
068-C2

DISCARD